From the Sea

Heather Hammonds

Contents

Rigby®

A World of Water

From space, planet Earth is mostly blue.
This is because almost three-quarters of
Earth is covered by water. Most of this
water is seawater.

The seas are very important. They are home to millions of plants and animals. Millions of plants in the sea make a gas called **oxygen**, which most living things need to survive. The seas also provide food and other important products to people, plants, and animals.

Without Earth's seas, life on Earth could not survive.

Beneath the Waves

Earth's seas are more than just water and waves. Beneath the waves, there are rocky reefs and tall mountains.

There are seaweed forests and deep dark caves—and millions of sea plants and animals!

The Great Barrier Reef, in northern Australia, is home to thousands of small coral. They need sunlight and warm **tropical** water to survive.

Coral looks like a plant, but it is really an animal! Most coral live together in a group called a colony.

Orcas, also known as killer whales, hunt for seals in the sea near Antarctica. Orcas and seals have a layer of **blubber** beneath their skin that keeps them warm in the icy Antarctic waters.

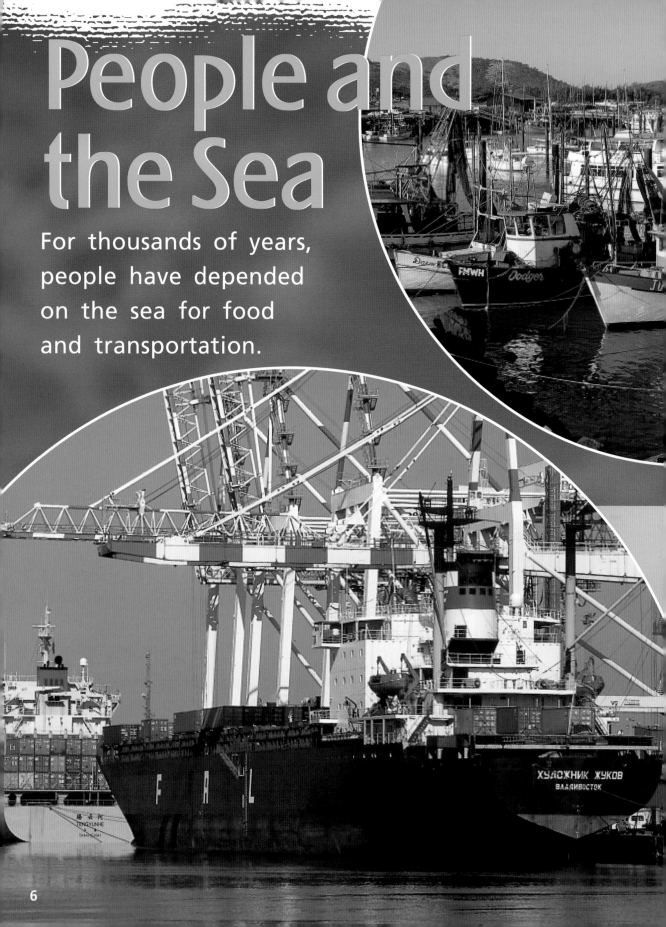

People and the Sea

For thousands of years, people have depended on the sea for food and transportation.

Sea plants and animals are an important source of food. Many people earn money and make a living by **harvesting** and selling these kinds of food.

Ships travel across the seas, carrying people and goods from country to country.

Around 80% of the goods traded around the world are carried by ships!

Oxygen from the Sea

Millions of tiny plants called **phytoplankton** live in the sea. Phytoplankton are very important. They make a gas called oxygen. Most living things on Earth need oxygen to survive.

Like land plants, phytoplankton use sunlight to make their own food. This is called **photosynthesis**.

A close-up of phytoplankton through a microscope.

Phytoplankton and other tiny sea creatures are also an important food source for some sea animals.

When phytoplankton make their own food, they also make oxygen. Without phytoplankton in the seas, there would be less oxygen in the air to breathe.

Food from the Sea

Fish make up much of the food harvested from the sea. Fishing boats travel to different **fishing grounds** to harvest fish.

Some fishing boats are very large. They catch thousands of fish and store them in big freezers before bringing them back to market.

Other types of animals are also harvested from the sea.

Lobsters, crabs, and other shellfish are caught in special traps.

Around 90 million tons of fish and shellfish are harvested each year from the sea. That's a lot of fish!

Divers collect **abalone** from rocks in the sea.

Traditional Fishing

Most seafood is harvested using modern methods. But some cultures still use **traditional** methods to catch fish.

Australian Aborigines hunt sea turtles. They hunt only what they and their families need to eat. They do not sell the turtles they catch.

Aquaculture

In some places, sea animals and seaweed are raised in special sea farms. This is called aquaculture.

Around 15 million tons of fish and shellfish are harvested in aquaculture farms every year.

Seaweed

Seaweed is a type of **algae**. Seaweed is harvested from the sea or grown on seaweed farms.

Some seaweeds are good to eat. Nori is a delicious seaweed. It is grown on farms in Japan. After nori is harvested, it is dried and pressed into sheets.

Nori

Kelp is a type of large seaweed. It is grown on seaweed farms or collected from the beach. Kelp is used to make many different products.

Kelp is used to make shampoo and ice cream.

Salt from the Sea

Seawater is too salty for people to drink, but the salt in sea water can be harvested.

In some countries, seawater is pumped into large ponds. The hot sun slowly **evaporates** the seawater. The ponds become saltier and saltier. Finally, all the seawater is gone. All that is left behind is the salt! This salt is called solar salt.

A pile of solar salt

Solar salt ponds

Salt is used in cooking, animal foods, and many other products.

Salt is used in peanut butter.

Animals also need salt. This cow is licking a block of salt.

Jewels from the Sea

Pearls come from pearl oysters.

Divers collect the oysters from the sea and take them to special farms.

At the farms, a tiny piece of shell or other material is placed inside the oyster. The material **irritates** the oyster. The oyster then begins to form a shiny coating around the material. This shiny coating becomes a pearl!

The oysters are cared for at the farm, while the pearls inside them grow bigger. After many months, the pearls are removed from the oysters.

Fuel and Power from the Sea

In some parts of the world, oil and natural gas are found beneath the seafloor.

Giant platforms are attached to the seafloor. Deep wells are drilled to collect the oil and natural gas. Pipes or ships carry the oil and natural gas back to land.

An oil rig drills for oil.

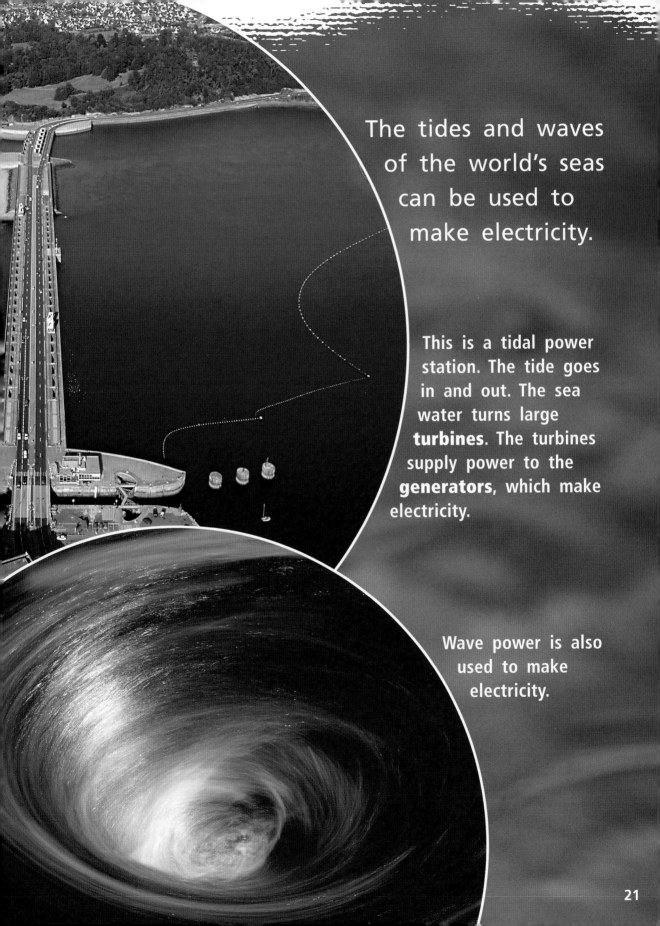

The tides and waves of the world's seas can be used to make electricity.

This is a tidal power station. The tide goes in and out. The sea water turns large **turbines**. The turbines supply power to the **generators**, which make electricity.

Wave power is also used to make electricity.

Caring for the Sea

The world's seas are very large, but they can be harmed by **pollution** and overfishing.

Some species of fish are close to extinction. It is important not to overfish endangered species.

Pollution is dangerous to sea plants and animals. It is dangerous to people, too!

Seas are an important **resource**. Conservation groups are working hard to protect the seas of the world.

The Southern blue-fin tuna is endangered. More than 11,000 tons of this fish are taken from the ocean every year.

Glossary

abalone a type of shellfish that lives in the sea

algae plant-like living things, found on land and in water. Seaweed is a type of algae.

blubber a layer of fat in some sea animals, such as the whale, that keeps them warm in icy waters

conservation groups organized groups of people that care for Earth

endangered in danger of being extinct

evaporates dries up

fishing grounds places where fish are caught

generators machines that make electricity

harvesting collecting crops or food

irritates annoys or disturbs

oxygen a gas that people, animals, and plants need to survive

photosynthesis the way green plants use light to make their own food

phytoplankton tiny plants that live in the sea

pollution harmful materials that damage Earth

resource something that supplies us with food or other important things

traditional doing something in the same way that it has been done for a very long time

tropical very warm, humid

turbines large machines used at power stations to make electricity

Index